Tips

for Graduates

Live a Fantastic Life!

By Gail Cassidy

Disclaimer and Terms of Use:

The Author and Publisher has strived to be as
accurate and complete as possible in the creation of
this book, notwithstanding the fact that he does not
warrant or represent at any time that the contents
within are accurate due to the rapidly changing
nature of the Internet. While all attempts have been
made to verify information provided in this
publication, the Author and Publisher assume no
responsibility for errors, omissions, or contrary
interpretation of the subject matter herein. Any
perceived slights of specific persons, peoples, or
organizations are unintentional.

Printed in the United States of America, First Printing,

Tomlyn Publications
547 Shackamaxon Drive
Westfield, NJ 07090

http://www.coachability.com

Tips

for Graduates

Live a Fantastic Life!

Table of Contents

Dear Graduate,

Life has its ups and down, but remember one very important fact: Our perspective and our state of mind create our reality. To give you a silly, but apt example from a Hallmark card, "To her lover, a beautiful woman is a delight; to a monk, she's a distraction; to a mosquito, a good meal." Everything in life depends on how you look at it. When in doubt, step into another person's shoes.

Every Spring, President Clinton speaks to thousands of graduating seniors in commencement ceremonies across the country, providing advice to graduates on how to pursue their dreams while also working together to combat the challenges facing our independent world. Below are excerpts from one of his addresses.

1. No matter what you do next, find ways to appreciate, celebrate, and enhance the impact of our diversity. Remember that our common humanity matters more than our interesting differences.

2. Take time to help others, in your own community or on another continent. You'll help build a world with more partners and fewer adversaries.

3. Engage respectfully with those you disagree with, and know that healthy debate can lead to positive changes. Remember that no matter what side of the argument you fall on, we're all in this future together.

4. You're going to be affected by things that happen to you beyond your borders, whether you like it or not. So try to work to build up the positives and reduce the negative forces of our interdependence.

5. Never forget your teachers and what they've done to make your life better and stronger. Even if you don't become a teacher yourself, remember their example, and try always to teach others and give the gift of learning.

6. Become an informed citizen. Engage with both local and global issues, and vote for leaders who you think are making a difference. Our world is filled with inequalities and instabilities, but that doesn't mean we all can't work together to change it.

7. When you're just starting out, you may not be making much money or be exactly where you expected, but there's always something you can do to give back. And doing good guarantees you a rewarding future.

8. Always try, and if you fail, try harder. Life's largest disappointments are not rooted in failures or mistakes, but in the absence of passionate commitment and effort.

9. Waste not a moment. Live your dreams. But find some way to empower other people to live theirs, too.

10. Strive to achieve happiness every day, not just at the end of a journey.

Whether you graduated yesterday or a decade ago, whether you're in the middle of a career or just starting out, we hope our advice inspires you to build a stronger tomorrow — and that you share this inspiration with others.

When dealing with people of any age, please remember Tip #1, See the invisible tattoo on every human being's forehead that reads: **"PLEASE MAKE ME FEEL IMPORTANT."**

Enjoy reading the Top Ten Lists and the Tips. Highlight those you want to keep in the forefront of your mind. Enjoy every day of your life. Each one holds a surprise for you. Look for it and when you find it, write it down, keep it forever.

I know of no one who deserves a great life than you. You possess all the ingredients for success!!

I wish you all the best in life!!!
Gail Cassidy

MAY YOUR LIFE BE FANTASTIC!

GENERAL PHILOSOPHY OF LIVING

1. See the invisible tattoo on everyone's forehead that reads: **"PLEASE MAKE ME FEEL IMPORTANT."**

2. Find at least one happening in each day to be grateful for.

3. Look for positives in every person.

4. Recognize the specialness of diversity.

5. Provide an atmosphere conducive to happiness, e.g. pictures, lighting, comfort, simplicity, etc.

6. Vary your daily activities. Do something different that will revitalize you.

7. Remember, humans of any age need breaks.

8. Know that everyone you meet has something special to offer.

9. Living in the moment is where you find happiness.

10. Learn the Serenity Prayer: "God, grant me the serenity to accept the things I cannot change, courage to change the things I can and the wisdom to know the difference."

11. "See" and/or "feel" your positive day before you climb out of bed. Use positive self talk.

12. Be (or act) enthusiastic about everything you do. It's contagious; it carries over to the people in your life.

13. Accept people as they are, and then provide the atmosphere for them be happy and grow.

14. Learn from every colleague, every friend.

15. Ask yourself, "Does it really matter?"

16. Being right does not always work, e.g.,
     Here lies the body of William Jay, who died
     maintaining his right of way. He was right,
     dead right as he sped along, but he's just as
     dead as if he were wrong.

17. HAVE FUN!

ATTITUDE

18. Park your ego at the door; it hinders relationships with co-workers and family.

19. Give your co-workers and family a reason to check their negative attitudes at the door also.

20. Know that people "mirror" you. They reflect what they see, hear, and feel from you.

21. Shake things up. Make changes. "If you always do what you have always done, you'll always get what you've always got."

22. Show people through your own example what fun having a great attitude is.

23. Be patient.

24. Positive attitudes are catching wherever you are.

25. Show respect to get respect.

26. Know that attitude is a choice everyone makes every day.

27. Explain that people cannot help what happens to them, but they are <u>always</u> in charge of their responses.

28. Remember, there is a pause between stimulus and response. Choose your response carefully.

29. Ask yourself why you are <u>choosing</u> to be unhappy, bored, tired, sad, happy.

30. Know that attitude is the steering mechanism of the brain. Body language can lead to attitude.

31. Practice changing your attitude by sitting or standing straight, with your head up and a smile on your face. It does work!

32. Know that it is the attitude of our hearts and minds that shape who we are, how we live, and how we treat others.

33. Help friends and family to recognize their specialness.

34. Success is feeling good about yourself every single day. That is attitude.

35. Know and share with your friends and family that true power is knowing that you can control your attitude at all times.

HUMAN RELATIONS

36. Treat everyone as if he or she were your friend's best friend.

37. Never talk down to anyone.

38. Find what is special about every person you meet.

39. **SMILE.** It warms a room.

40. Use tact when responding to a challenging person. The rewards outweigh "being right."

41. Know that it is not okay for people to feel your negativity. That is your choice.

42. Be 100% fair at all times--no exceptions.

43. Keep in mind that perception is reality--yours and your friends and family's.

44. Treat every person as you wish to be treated.

45. Understand that no one <u>wants</u> to be wrong.

46. Everyone desperately wants to feel special.

47. Remember that people gravitate toward things that are pleasurable and avoid things that are painful. Make learning pleasurable.

48. **LISTENING** is the greatest compliment.

49. Try to understand before being understood.

50. Show genuine appreciation to people you work and live with.

51. Begin corrective action with sincere and honest recognition of what has been done correctly.

52. Never embarrass anyone. Allow the person to save face.

53. Use encouragement. Make the error seem easy to correct.

54. Don't be afraid to admit your mistakes. It will make you appear more human.

55. Show respect for every person's opinion.

56. Challenge people to be the best that they can be.

57. Make **SINCERITY** your No. 1 priority.

COMMUNICATION

58. Set standards in your everyday life and share them with your friends and family.

59. Know the purpose and importance of what you are doing.

60. Set high expectations.

61. Know that 55% of all messages comes from the body. Notice how you can tell your special someone is in a bad mood without any words being spoken.

62. Know that 38% of the message comes from the voice: inflection, intonation, pitch, speed, e.g., "I didn't say he stole the exam." Seven words = seven meanings.

63. Know, you cannot **NOT** communicate.

64. Recognize that we don't all see the same thing when looking at the same thing.

65. Know also that we don't all hear the same things even when listening to the same words.

66. Control your thoughts; your feelings come from your thoughts; therefore, you can also control your feelings! Choice is control.

67. Take responsibility for what you say and how you say it.

68. Listen for the message, yet know that body language can be interpreted as only a clue to the meaning of the message, e.g., arms crossed in front of chest could mean blocking you or it could mean the person is actually cold or comfortable.

69. Learn to lead rather than to try and overcome resistance.

70. Communicate your enthusiasm through your body and voice.

71. "One who is too insistent on his own views, find few to agree with him." -Lao-Tze

72. Speak with a warm heart.

SELF ESTEEM

73. Know that a person with high self-esteem does not need to find fault with others.

74. Remember that people find fault with others when they feel threatened, consciously or unconsciously.

75. Know that self-esteem is not noisy conceit. It is a quiet sense of self-respect, a feeling of self-worth. Conceit is whitewash to cover low self-esteem.

76. Remember, people have two basic needs: to know they are lovable and worthwhile.

77. Remember, it is a person's feeling about being respected or not respected that affects how s/he will behave and perform.

78. Helping people build their self concept is key to being a successful parent and/or friend.

79. Know that your words have power to affect a person's self-esteem.

80. Each person values himself to the degree s/he has been valued.

81. Words are less important in their affect on self-esteem than the judgments that accompany them.

82. The attitude of others toward a person's capacities is more important than his possession of particular traits.

83. Bragging people are asking for positive reflections.

84. Masks are worn to hide the "worthless me."

85. Low self-esteem is tied to impossible demands on the self.

86. A person's own self-acceptance frees him or her to focus on others, unencumbered by inner needs.

87. The single most important ingredient in a nurturing relationship is honesty.

88. Ask this: "If I were to treat my friends as I treat my children, how many friends would I have left?"

89. Avoid mixed messages. Be clear in your statements of expectations.

BOUNDARIES

90. Tolerate no disrespect.

91. Be consistent in enforcing rules.

92. Set boundaries.

93. Find opportunities for each others to improve the quality of his/her work.

94. Differentiate between the action and the person.

95. Uncover and address, when possible, the reasons for the person's poor performance.

96. Make sure people you work with have the skills to succeed.

97. Focus, as often as possible, on what is right rather than what is wrong.

98. Give plenty of recognition for the unique gifts of each person.

99. Keep in mind that you have power in the present moment to change your thoughts, feelings, and attitude about the past.

100. Take control of your life by focusing on the present.

101. Remove the word "try" from your vocabulary. "Try" to pick up a pencil. Either you do or you don't.

102. Find the lesson or value in unacceptable situations.

103. Know that you have choices in spite of your past experiences.

104. Turn problems into a learning opportunity.

105. Have a clear vision of where you are going.

106. Approach problematic situations with relaxed confidence.

107. Respond thoughtfully to challenging and/or problem situations.

108. Avoid making judgments.

109. Learn problem solving:
- State the problem
- Look for causes of the problem
- Brainstorm solutions
- Choose the best one

110. Always see beyond your own point of view.

111. Encourage habits of thought conducive to growth in understanding others, to think outside the box.

112. Recognize that there is no one interpretation of text.

LIFE'S TREASURE TIPS

113. Begin to be now what you will be hereafter.
- St. Jerome. Repetition is the mother of skill.

114. Know that you too are special.

115. Enjoy each day and each moment of life.

116. Make corrections by citing two positives for every negative.

117. Live in the present.

118. Be alert for moments of gratitude.

119. Show lively enthusiasm!

120. Create an atmosphere of fun.

121. Build on successes.

122. Create a routine with varied activities.

123. Turn people on to learning.

124. Visualize doing well.

125. Be relaxed.

126. Make everyone feel important.

127. Remember, "You are what you choose today." -Dyer.

128. Give yourself opportunities to succeed.

129. Provide a safe atmosphere.

130. Validate yourself frequently.

131. Your reality is what you make it to be.

132. Polish your people skills.

133. Hone your communications skills.

134. Take excellent care of yourself.

MORE TIPS

135. Work towards feeling good about yourself. It is man's highest goal.

136. Always do what you feel is right or true.

137. Your actions reveal your values.

138. Your thought is the most powerful force in your universe. "Nothing is either good or bad but thinking makes it so." -Shakespeare.

139. Whatever you dwell on expands.

140. Work toward goals that cause you to feel a sense of mastery.

141. Write a list of everything you have accomplished or have been recognized for in your life. Add to it whenever you think of something new. Read it when the going gets tough.

142. Have a clear sense of purpose in life.

143. Clarify your goals and focus on them

144. Be a risk taker. Step outside your comfort zone. Try something new.

145. Positive expectations are the single, most outwardly identifiable, characteristics all successful people possess.

146. You can train yourself to think more positively by training yourself to choose what you pay attention to and what you say about it, both to yourself and others. "We know what we are but know not what we may be." -Shakespeare.

147. Whatever you believe, picture in your mind, and think about most of the time, you eventually will bring into reality.

148. Your self-image is the most dominant factor that affects everything you attempt to do.

149. Nothing is more exciting than the realization that you can accomplish anything you really want that is consistent with your unique mix of natural talents and abilities.

150. Remember, "Change your thoughts and you change your world." -Norman Vincent Peale.

WORTHY QUOTES

- Assume a virtue, if you have it not.
  - Shakespeare.

- Act enthusiastic and you'll be enthusiastic.
  - Carnegie.

- It is not the place, nor the condition, but the mind alone that can make any one happy or miserable. - L Estrange.

- Beliefs have the power to create and the power to destroy. -Robbins.

- Nothing is more likely to help a person overcome or endure troubles than the consciousness of having a task in life. - Frankl.

- When the student is ready, the teacher will appear. - Zen proverb.

- The ancestor to every action is a thought.
  - Emerson.

29

- Imagination is more important than knowledge. - Albert Einstein.

- Things do not change; we change. - Thoreau.

- Great men are those who see that thoughts rule the world. - Emerson.

- Nothing has any power over me other than that which I give it through my conscious thoughts. - Anthony Robbins.

- The greatest discovery of my generation is that human beings can alter their lives by altering their attitudes of mind. -William James.

- The only limits you have are the limits you believe. - Wayne Dyer.

- Anything we fail to reinforce will eventually dissipate. - Robbins.

- Patience is the companion of wisdom.
  - Augustine.

- The more he gives to others, the more he possesses of his own. -Lao-Tze.

- Vision is the art of seeing things invisible. – Swift.

- Believing is seeing. - Dyer.

- I don't know the key to success, but the key to failure is trying to please everybody. – Bill Cosby

- Failure is the key to success; each mistake teaches us something. – Morihei Ueshiba

- Success is not the key to happiness. Happiness is the key to success. If you love what you are doing, you will be successful. – Albert Scheiwitzer

- The key to success is to focus our conscious mind on things we desire not things we fear. – Brian Tracy

- The key to success is to keep growing in all areas of life – mental, emotional, spiritual, as well as physical. – Julius Erving

- One important key to success is self-confidence. An important key to self-confidence is preparation. – Arthur Ashe

- Education is the key to success in life, and teachers make a lasting impact in the lives of their students. – Solomon Ortiz

- I always say be humble but be firm. Humility and openness are the key to success without compromising your beliefs. – George Hickenlooper

- Before anything else, preparation is the key to success. – Alexander Graham Bell

- A graduation ceremony is an event where the commencement speaker tells thousands of students dressed in identical caps and gowns that "individuality" is the key to success.
  – Robert Orben

- Focused, hard work is the real key to success. Keep your eyes on the goal, and just keep taking the next step towards completing it. If you aren't sure which way to do something, do it both ways and see which works better.
  – John Carmack

- Positive thinking is the key to success in business, education, pro football, anything that you can mention. I go out there thinking that

I'm going to complete every pass. – Ron
Jaworski

- That's the key to success, isn't it? It has to be
fun. – Monica Seles

- Dear disgruntled artists: the key to success
isn't kicking down the door; it's building your
own. – Brian Cello

[From BrainyQuote.com]

- "You have brains in your head. You have feet in
your shoes. You can steer yourself in any
direction you choose. You're on your own. And
you know what you know. You are the guy
who'll decide where to go. – Dr. Seuss

- "Do not go where the path may lead; go
instead where there I no path and leave a
trail." – Ralph Waldo Emerson

- "I hope your dreams take you…to the corners
of your smiles, to the highest of your hopes, to
the windows of your opportunities, and to the
most special places your heart has ever
known." – unknown

- "The future belong to those who believe in the beauty of their dreams." – Eleanor Roosevelt

- "To accomplish great things, we must not only act, but also dream; not only plan, but also believe." – Anatole France

- "Go confidently in the direction of your dreams. Life the life you have imagined." – Henry David Thoreau

- "Success is the ability to go from one failure to another with no loss of enthusiasm." – Winston Churchill

- "All our dreams can com true…if we have the courage to pursue them." - Walt Disney

- "Go for it now. The future is promised to no one." – Wayne Dyer

- "If you can imagine it, you can achieve it; if you can dream it, you can become it." – William Arthur Ward

- "What lies behind us and what lies before us are tiny matters compared to what lies within us." – Ralph Waldo Emerson

- "Education is the most powerful weapon which you can use to change the world." – Nelson Mandela

- "Don't judge each day by the harvest you reap but by the seeds that you plants." – Robert Louis Stevenson

- "Time is not measured by the passing of years but by what one does, what one feels, and what one achieves." – Jawaharial Nehru

- "If opportunity doesn't knock, build a door." – Milton Berle

- "Graduation day is tough for adults. They go to the ceremony as parents. They come home as contemporaries. After twenty-two years of child-raising, they are unemployed." –Erma Bombeck

- "Dream no small dreams for they have no power to move the hearts of men." - Johann Wolfgang von Goethe

- "There is a good reason they call these ceremonies 'commencement exercises'. Graduation is not the end, it's the beginning." - Orrin Hatch

- "Nothing happens unless first a dream." –Carl Sandburg

- "Your schooling may be over, but remember that your education still continues."
  – unknown

- "The human spirit needs to accomplish, to achieve, to triumph to be happy." – Ben Stein

[from Thinkexist.com'

- "Be who you are and say what you feel, because those who mind don't matter and those who matter don't mind." - Dr. Seuss

FAVORITE TOP TEN LISTS

The Top 10 Ways to Create the Life of Your Dreams

We all deserve to live a happy, fulfilling life. YOU and only you have the power to make that happen. Here are some steps to get you started.

1. Be quiet!

Take time to listen to your spirit, your inner voice, whatever you choose to call it. We get too caught up in the day-to-day stresses and obligations in our lives. Get quiet and tune in to who you really are.

2. Find a passion.

Everyone needs to find a passion, but as I stated in number one we are often so over stressed that we don't have a clue to what our passion may be. Here's a start: Take five minutes and write down everything that you love - partners and kids excluded - (we KNOW you love them!)

3. Find your spirit.

Life needs to have balance - mind, body and spirit. It's like a three legged stool - with only two legs, or one, it falls over. It doesn't have to be organized religion, it's whatever fills your spirit - a walk on the beach, a hike in the woods, meditation, prayer. Find the force that is bigger than you.

4. Be grateful.

I am like a broken record with this - but it's true. Life is always richer when we have appreciation for what we have in our life.

5. Give to others.

Giving of yourself is always a great way to give to yourself. It's a win-win situation! Find a cause, a neighbor who's lonely, an animal shelter where they need someone to walk the dogs. It will fill your spirit - just try it!

6. Create intentions and affirmations.

Write down what you want to come in to your life - be specific and positive. Don't use language like "want" - as in "I want a great job." Use a present tense - "I have a job that is fulfilling that I love." It can really work if you say them everyday!

7. Become selfish.

By taking more time to care for yourself you bring more happiness and peace to your life. By loving yourself enough to take care of you, you have more energy and love to give to others.

8. Work on your thoughts.

The most powerful tool you have to change your life is your own thoughts. You can change the way you think to be more loving toward yourself, to be happier, and more at peace. Every time you have a negative thought STOP and replace it with a positive one.

9. Take time every day to DO something you love.

Make sure you enjoy yourself everyday. Dance, paint, laugh, whatever makes YOU feel wonderful!

10. Get support!

It's not easy to change; it takes determination. Find a friend, hire a coach, get someone who understands what you are trying to do. Life can be a wonderful adventure - it's never too late unless you don't get started!

[Originally submitted by Candace Hammond, Coach University Graduate, Personal and Life Coach, who can be reached at mantis@capecod.net]

The Top 10 Rules for the Game of Life

We have all been given our precious life. How can you take yours to the next level of happiness? Start by realizing the following:

1. Life is NOT a Game.

There is no dress rehearsal.

2. This is YOUR life.

This is not somebody else's life. Do what you really want to do. Learn to put yourself first.

3. You no longer have to live by shoulda's, coulda's, oughta's or if only's.

Live in the present and make each day perfect for you. Have no preoccupations with your past or future. Don't let others' beliefs that don't work for you determine how you will live your life.

4. There is no such thing as TRYing.

Simply put, there is really no trying--either you do it or you don't. Put your arms down in front of you; now try to lift your arm. Did you do it? My point is that either you lifted you arm or you didn't. Trying is not full effort and doesn't portray your commitment.

5. Success is what YOU define it to be.

If you believe you are successful, you are. Success is measured in numerous ways. If you are intrinsically successful then it would be very difficult not to let

6. YOU are perfect just the way YOU are.

Stop focusing on your shortcomings. Start loving yourself and your uniqueness and special gifts.

7. Listen to YOUR inner wisdom.

It is this voice or intuition that helps guide you and your decisions.

8. There are many lessons to be learned.

There is a lesson to be learned in every triumph as well as every failure. Look for the lessons.

9. You need to have a vision.

Having a vision is the first step toward having the life you want. Purpose gives meaning to your life and changes your attitude and perspective about life.

10. YOU must take actions.

If you want a more satisfying, fulfilling and balanced life, you must begin taking actions to create it. Status quo is not good enough when you have a gap between where you are and where you want to be. Set goals to support your vision and your dreams. Focus on results and if you're not getting the results you want, find the reason.

[Originally submitted by Natalie A. Gahrmann, M.A., Coach U Graduate, and author, who can be reached at nataliegahrmann@hotmail.com]

The Top 10 Principles to Achieving a Life Beyond Balance

Recognition that words like balance or juggling don't fit is finally here! Switching off at work about what is happening at home and putting life into pockets is meaningless. It requires sacrifice or conflict. The beautiful integrated, flowing, harmonious way that people wish to live is beyond this. This Top Ten gives tips for achieving a fulfilled and guilt free life, without sacrificing the people or things you love.

1. Design the life you want.

It seems obvious, but it is easier to say what you don't want. Make a clear statement to yourself about the life you want. Be specific. Every day take one step towards achieving that dream - focus on what is possible, not what is impossible. Say no to what you don't want.

2. Know what your values are.

Think of a time when you felt honored, fulfilled, and happy and describe this to yourself or a friend. Listen to how your values show up and from today do nothing that would dishonor these. Ask - what is the cost to me of not honoring my values?

3. Live your life fully in the moment.

Be present in every moment, conversation and relationship you have. Know that when you forget this, you lose so much time and energy it is catastrophic. You can waste a day wondering what to do next, instead of enjoying what you are doing. Watch your children - they are experts.

4. Value your dream time.

Spend moments just wandering in your head or physically visit the place you dream you will live in or hang out. Gather pictures of what this future will be like. Behave like the person you want to be. Make your dreams real. Now.

5. Know what your limits are.

Putting up with things about yourself, the way people treat you, your environment, and your possessions uses up energy that would be better spent else where. Set these limits selfishly!

6. Chose how you will be.

I am self-conscious, untalented, unworthy, too busy......No! Say, "Until now I have chosen to be self-conscious, untalented., unworthy, too busy, and from today I chose to be confident, talented, worthy, and live my life at the pace I love"

7. Know what might stop you.

Identify the things that you know might stop you and be ready for them. Identify what you might do to sabotage this process and who might get in your way. Prepare, notice and react positively.

8. Have a support network.

Someone who supports you in your dreams and aspirations and is there for you when you need a friendly face is essential for this to work. A coach, a partner or a friend will keep you on track and encourage you when things get tough.

9. Make now the right time to start.

Listen to yourself say - "This will work when I have more money/time/space/when the kids have grown up.......Give it up! Phrase the things you desire in the here and now

10. Start now.

Have a handful of things that you do every day that are just for you - a good cappuccino, a hot bath, time with your children. This will nurture you and remind you of the commitment you have made to having a beautiful integrated, flowing, harmonious, wonderful, fulfilled life that is YOURS!!

[Originally submitted by Mairi Watson, Founder partner of Professional Life Coaching, Life Coach, who can be reached at mairi@professionallifecoaching.com]

The Top 10 Steps to a Successful Life

1. Make your intuition your ally.

How does your intuition speak to you? Do you receive information in words, feelings, a body sensation? Do you just know? Ask your intuition questions and pay attention to the answers and act on the information you receive.

2. What are you enthusiastic about?

The root of the word enthusiasm is entheos. It literally means "God Within." Just think, when you feel enthusiastic about your dreams it means that God is speaking through you and saying "yes" to your goals! The feeling of enthusiasm is one of the ways your intuition speaks to you. What makes you excited, happy, delighted? What do you look forward to each day? Do more of it!

3. Be clear about your goals.

We are often quite clear about what we don't want. Spend time thinking about what you do want. What does your ideal life look like? Draw pictures or cut out scenes from magazines that illustrate the life you want to create. Write in your journal, envision. Spend time each day imagining your ideal life. Envision the details of that life. Imagine you are living it now. What are you wearing? What are you feeling? Who are the people around you? The power is within your mind and heart to bring forth the new life you want.

4. Spend time in prayer and meditation.

Answers often come to life's questions through self-reflection. Prayer and meditation are two ways we have of slowing down enough to listen to the still, quiet voice of our Higher Self. Remember that the answers don't always pop into your mind fully formed as you meditate or pray. You may find them slowly evolving into your consciousness over several days or weeks as you ask for insight.

5. Create positive self-talk.

Pay attention to what you tell yourself about yourself and your life. If the general tone is hopeful and positive you feel better and are more optimistic. William James said, "The greatest discovery of my generation is that human beings, by changing the inner attitudes of their minds, can change the outer aspects of their lives." It's easier to create a life you love when you give yourself affirmative message.

6. Practice an attitude of gratitude.

Research has shown that the happiest people are the ones who have gratitude for all that they have despite their circumstances. You don't have to postpone happiness until you have achieved all your goals. Joy is an inside job. In the Talmud it says, "In the world to come each of us will be called to account for all the good things God put on this earth which we refused to enjoy." Learn to appreciate the unfolding process of your life, not just the realization of your dreams.

7. Take action.

People often get stuck because they can't figure out how to get from Point A to Point Z. What is one thing you could do that would be a next step? Take a class, talk to a friend, read a book on a topic of interest, learn a new skill. Take action on what feels exciting to you.

8. Look for coincidences and synchronicities.

It has been said that coincidences are God's way of remaining anonymous. We often have serendipity occurring in our lives as a way to show us we are on the right path. As you trust your intuitive knowing you'll find these synchronicities occurring more often.

9. Know that there will be ebbs and flows.

We often reach success through a series of ups and downs. When you are in a "down" place and feeling stuck, know that it won't last forever. Find some ways to enjoy your life despite the lull and continue to focus on what you want.

10. Trust in divine order.

Maybe you're beginning to feel as Mother Theresa once did when she said, "I know God will not give me anything I can't handle. I just wish that He didn't trust me so much." The Universe has a perfect plan for your growth and unfolding as a human being. As you learn to be guided by your intuition you're beginning to act on this wisdom from the Universe.

[Originally submitted by Lynn A. Robinson, who can be reached at Lynn@lynnrobinson.com.]

The Top 10 Rules for Creating a Better Life

It's said that it's the simple things in life that truly give our lives meaning. Here are 10 tips for creating that better life:

1. Count your blessings daily.

Even with life's challenges, there are always positive things, people, and events in our lives that keep us going. Make a list of those things in your life that keep you fueled, and give thanks for them daily.

2. Do more than you are getting paid to do.

Going the extra mile brings many unexpected rewards into our life. Remind yourself that it's a privilege to be able to add value to someone else's life.

3. Shake off your blunders.

Whenever you get knocked down by life, don't look back on it too long. Mistakes are life's greatest teachers; they help us grow and move on to higher planes, but only if we remain unstuck.

4. Reward yourself in the best way you can after a period of long labor and achievement.

Stretch your reward by sharing it with someone special.

5. Remember that you are God's perfect creation; you can do anything you dream of anytime you want.

6. Let your actions always speak of your values.

Be on guard for false pride and deceit that may halt your progress.

7. Every day should be unwrapped as a precious gift.

Life may offer hurdles and stumbling blocks; use these as stepping stones to reaching your goal.

8. Live this day as if it were your last.

Today is all you have. Run with it!

9. Extend everyone you meet all the care, kindness, love, and understanding you can muster, without thought of reward.

Give of yourself: your time, your money, your talent or skills. Take the focus off yourself. Your life will never be the same.

10. Laugh at yourself and at life.

Laughing causes a release of tension and worry, and clears your mind to think clearly toward a solution that is certain to come as soon as you let go.

[Originally submitted by Carmen Stine, Personal Development & Media Coach, who can be reached at coachmentor@aol.com]

The Top 10 Ways To Go for It!

When I ask people to list reasons why we hold back and stop short of reaching our goals and living our dreams, the reasons usually involve fear--fear of failure, fear of success, fear of rejection, fear of not being good enough, fear of looking foolish.

We've all heard that FEAR stands for False Evidence Appearing Real. Here are 10 things you can do to get control of your FEARS and Fully Eliminate All Roadblocks to Success.

1. Listen to your heart.

Norman Vincent Peale wrote that when you have a desire for something that won't go away, that's the voice of God saying that's what you should do. Your heart holds the issues of your life. Listen to it.

2. Dream big.

A client of mine was once driving to Atlanta in her Pugeot. It was a nice car but she wanted a Mercedes, even though she couldn't quite afford it yet. She had a thought accompanied by a strong feeling that "the next time I drive to Atlanta I'll be driving my new

Mercedes." Sure enough, that's exactly what happened.

3. Have faith in yourself.

There is no one else on earth like you. Perhaps you want to write a book but don't think it's worth it because so many others have already written a book on your topic. You have a unique perspective that we need to hear. Even an expert can read your book and learn something from you. We're all teachers and we're all students.

4. Have faith in others.

Most people tend to worry too much about what other people think of them. It's your dream; it doesn't matter what others think you should have/be/do. And most people are pulling for you, especially if you're providing a service or product that helps them. They want you to succeed!

5. Have faith in God.

When I started my business, I had many moments of self-doubt and anxiety. How will I get clients? Will I make enough money to survive? One day a thought came to me; it was so strong it almost knocked me over. That thought was, "God got me this far, He won't drop me now." So whenever I have an anxious moment, I think about that, and am able to move forward with courage and faith.

6. Use positive self-talk.

When Moses asked God what His name was, He said, "I Am." What powerful words those are. And whatever adjectives we follow those two words with when describing ourselves will determine who and what we are. If you say, "I am afraid," you'll be afraid. If you say, "I am courageous," you'll be brave. The quality of our lives is determined by our consciousness. ACT successful, and you will be.

7. Visualize positive outcomes.

When pursuing a goal, imagine how success will look to you. What will you have, where will you be, who's with you? All the little details. If you're more kinesthetic than visual, imagine how you'll feel. And if you're more auditory, imagine the sounds of applause and praise you'll receive when you've gotten there and done a good job.

8. Ask, "Is it really too late?"

A woman in her forties wrote to Dear Abby and asked her advice about going to college at her age. It was an unfulfilled dream for her, but she thought she was too old. She said, "I'll be 48 when I graduate." Abby asked her, "And how old will you be then if you don't do it?"

9. Start with a small step.

How do you eat an elephant? One bite at a time. Any task, project, or goal can look almost impossibly huge when you're standing here and looking there. It's enough to make some people give up. You can do it by planning a strategy on how to get there, and writing down the steps with deadlines. When you do it one step at a time, it's much easier.

10. Hire a coach.

I probably wouldn't still be in business if it weren't for my coach. Going it alone is hard for even the most dedicated self-starter. A good coach will help you get organized and focused and will guide you to your goal, giving you praise and encouragement along the way. If not a coach, then find a mentor or really good friend who will walk with you all the way. Go For It! You deserve it! If anyone can do it, you can! [Originally submitted by Annette Estes, Certified Professional Behavioral and Values Analyst, Life Success Coach, who can be reached at aestes@mindspring.com.]

**What the mind can conceive
and believe, it can achieve.
-Napoleon Hill**

HAVE A GREAT LIFE!!!!